THE INVISIBLE MAN AND OTHER REALITIES

WRITTEN WORDS BY

DAWI OPARA

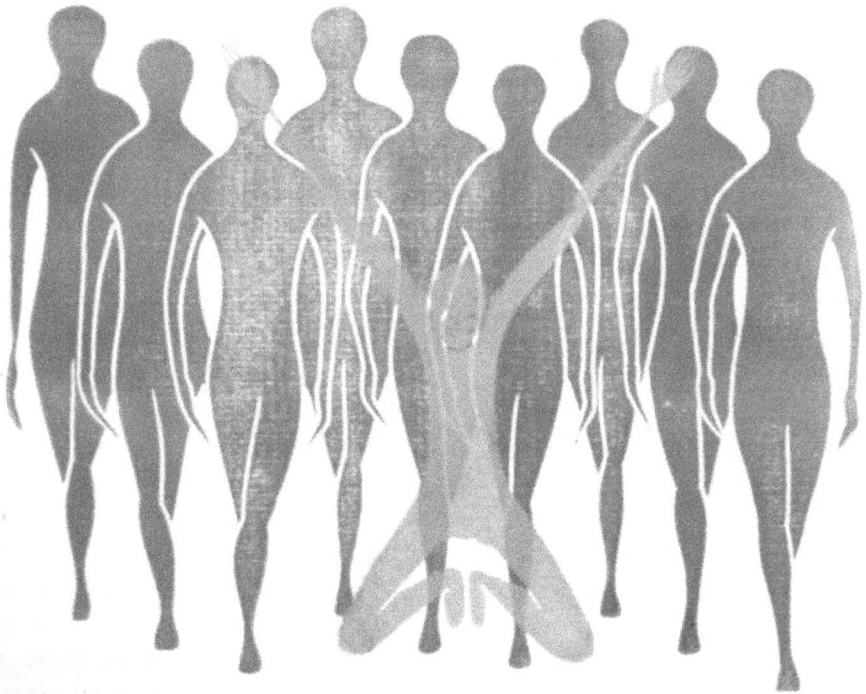

Illustrations by: Jeff McNear

INTRODUCTION

Dawi Opara offers treasures of inspiration, hopes and dreams for people of color, as well as those open enough to grasp his ideology. His work spans 30 years. Expressing the heritage of the past, as well as the challenges of the present and the promise of the future. Take the time to hear and read these words of wisdom. Take the time to feel the echo of these words. He lifts his voice to ease the pain; he lifts his voice to forge ahead. There is no doubt; the spoken and written word will provoke thoughts as intended, as the spoken and written word is meant. Whether whispered, or scrolled on bits of paper, born out of love or anger, wailed in anguish from a jail or church, they are most powerful.

T.A.S.
02-18-02

This book is dedicated to my mother Flossie,
And my woman Loretta .
All my children Ameer, Rahsaan, Ora, Ashanti,
Tyree, Naima, Sadeea, Dawud,
Kedar, Yusef, Saharah & Ameena.

I would like to give special thanks to Ameer.
Without his support, contribution, and telling me
"Man u better get up on computers".

I would like to give special thanks
to Douglas Ewart who simply told me
Do it man do it.
Thanks Douglas

And special thanks to Rah for proofing.

And last, but not least a special thanks goes out to 3
members of the Men's Art Forum:
Andy Mitran, Al Jewer and Jeff McNear.

Table of Contents

Works on Beauty

Butterfly   13
Earthbound   15
Twilight   17
Love   18
Quarter Mile from Insanity   20

Works on Common Emotion

Humid Heat   25
Tears   27
The Game   28
The Same   31
Waiting   33
Laughter   35
Last Times   36
Listen to her Scream   38
Merry Christmas   40
Arm to Disarm   42

Works on Women

Loneliness   47
Narcotics   49
To Touch You   50
B.B.W.   52
Chocolate Lady   55

Works on Creativity

The Artist   58
Music   60
Acting   63
She Dances   66
To Be the Creator   68
To Lovers who Dance   70
Stardust Dance   72

Works on Addiction

Addiction (the Comfort Zone)   76
Lady of the Night   79
Chronical   81

Works on the Struggle

Invisible Man   85
European American Blacknuss   87
House Niggers-N-Field Niggers   90
The Ship's Gut   92
U-Lie the 4th   95
Grabbing Myself   98
The Rainbow Coalition   101
Martin the King   103
U Done Come a Long Way Baby   105
One Saturday Morning   109

Works on Beauty

Butterfly

In a world of monetary madness.
We strive to live in New Eden.
Promoting fleeting butterfly wings of reality.
Colorful illusions of fragile failings.
With only dust remaining on fingertips.

Earth bound

Sailing on winds.
Birds gliding with ease of freedom.
I enjoy those visions of flight.
To fly and be among the clouds.
Melting wings of wax and feathers.
Drowned visions of free flight.
I can only dream.
Never soaring.
Looking up with envy.
Forever to be earthbound.

Twilight

Twilight, just before the changing of now.
Darkness of light prevails.
Soft glares of changing shadows that blankets all.
A state of mindless relaxation.
Glimmers of hope defining sleep for some.
Movement for others.
The order of opposition.
Man is not nocturnal.
Hope arises each day with the birth of the sun.
We creatures of adaptation.
Vessels of free will and determination.
Creatures who mimics the twilight.
Man is twilight, always changing just before the
changing of now.

Love

Love, an invisible elixir that bonds fusing us together.
Unseen electro chemical forces
of positive negative and neutral energy.
Invading the heart with magnetic stealth of light
accuracy.
Influencing the alpha and omega of human existence.
Love a gift from God.
When shared equally between two lovers.
It becomes energy of harmonious harmony.
When this gift is shared with no give and take.
It becomes a roller coaster ride.
That divides them with great clarity, into submission,
domination, or simply waging war in the declaration of
love.
Either harmonic or inharmonic chaos love it is non-
discriminating.
Taking our breaths away making our hearts flutter.
Sweating breathing erratically not knowing what to
say or do.
It is a feeling of complete nervous dizzy helplessness.
Yeah man ain't being in love a bitch.
Being in love at times can defy common sense of logic.
Turn one plus one into three an impossibility in any
reality.

Being in love can transform us into acts
beyond recognition of self.
Where nothing matters but the giving, taking or
equality of love.
Pushing us to the brink of self destruction.
Controlled by love for love.
Pushing us to heights of new horizons.
Controlled by love for love.
Love unconditional selfish or equal.
Simply a path chosen with three forks in the road.
Yeah man ain't being in love a bitch

Quarter Mile from Insanity

Concrete, steel, glass, lights the city.
Collisions of sounds verbalizing the hopes, the fears,
and the energies that fuels movements of humanity.
The hustle, the bustle, the good, the bad.
Countless entities moving about.
Moving forward with continuity, of logical insanity.
The city its thoughts move with rapid fluidity.
Day or night it shapes the shape of things to come.
Days cascading without end.
Infested with creative non-creative repetitive
investments
of mundane madness.
Reaping monetary rewards
equating levels of survival.
A nine to five for 20 to 35.
Looking for more than a gold watch.
Looking for more than a depleted 401-k plan.
Looking for more than some treachery of corporate
board absconding with pension funds.
Days are truly madness.
A daily game of making it to clock out time,
to the final clock out.
Yeah man we move to do, what we must do.
As we await the rotation of revolving earth.
Night.
Like vampires we come alive.
Licking wounds from the non-relenting pressure
 of regimented survival.

As darkness slowly soaks up daydreams of scaling
Everest. Absorbing the madness of daily repetition of
repetitions.
As we look for what is calmness.
Programmed we seek refuge looking for isolation of
inner peace within the population.
Looking for quiet solitude within the multitude.
Hoping, attempting to relax to recharge our souls.
To feel the energy of Quasimodo's screams for
Esmeralda.
Sanctuary, sanctuary, sanctuary.
A place where only you can invade.
A place where only you can invade.
But within the city I found a place,
tucked away, a quarter mile from insanity.
Away from the glaring bright lights,
noises and smells of man's movements.
A mini Eden so to speak.
With lushness of greenery,
the bountiful, beautiful odors of nature permeates
everywhere.
Day or night it is wonderful.
It is nature's narcotic peace.
The nights regardless of season are stunning and
hypnotic.
Awesome, rawsome beautiful.
No streetlights,
the sky becomes a pitch black canopy of sparkling,
blinking lights of far off constellations.
That still cloaks the mysteries of the universe.
Trees, pillars of centurions go from green to bare.

Allowing no one in but nature.
Guarding the peaceful fullness of emptiness.
With eyes closed the smells, the flutter of wings,
the rustle in the bush.
The rushing water of a river that never stops.
Sensory overload into Utopia.
Venting pressures of these robotic days.
No cold turkey, a soft, slow release of contained
pressure.
As nature relaxes and replenishes you with its
goodness,
it's essence of creation.
Remembering when time was not rigid or linear,
but one's perception of it.
Overloading into peaceful exhilaration of relaxation.
Becoming one with self.
Relaxing in the bosom of Nature,
a quarter mile from insanity.

Works on our Common Emotions

Humid Heat

Daytime, sun blasting, blazing.
Water thick in air.
Undergarments sticking in cracks and crevices.
Pulling them out as they sink back into cracks and
crevices of uncomfortable hot wet misery.
Breathing becomes a non-lethal miserable struggle to
attain air.
Even in darkness of night humidity reigns supreme.
Without motion sweat drips profusely.
As if the sun were blazing on u.
The breezes bringing hot flashes of hotter winds.
Sleep is impossible, tossing turning.
As skin, sticking to skin to sheets, to everything.
With the A.C. on the blink rotating fans simply adds
fuel to the fire.
With watery sweat dripping looking for a dry cool
spot.
Even getting naked offers no relief as liquid air pushes
lungs into overdrive.
Tomorrow's prediction.
No relief in sight.

Tears

I saw your tears falling and
I tried to catch them.
They exploded in my hands into nothingness.
Like the faded memories of us.

The Game

The game of life, a most intriguing endeavor.
A who did it that becomes, why was it done?
Individuality.
It is 5 billion strong and growing.
A diversity of plays and options beyond imagination.
It has no equal.
Its sophisticated tapestry of life is woven with trial
and error.
Leaving scars to remind us, that the game never
changes.
Only the players.
Even the sharpest of us can only play off what has
been left before.
Improvising the basics, the substance that makes
true game, game.
Game is mankind.
A compilation of lessons learned, relearned, modified.
Making change for a change, forever changing to stay
game.
Logic is deceptive game.
Individual interpretation is true game.
True game is more elusive than catching light.
Flashbacks flash forward, flash now.
A reflection of a reflection, reflecting back to itself,
to the truth.

And.

The game goes on.

It is neither positive nor negative, no will, only degrees of greed.

It's destiny, shaped by the desires of man.

It's reality, survival of the gamest.

Game is more than knowledge.

More than wisdom.

It is this combination that allows game to flow.

At one level or another.

We all become perpetrator, victim, or spectator.

Game is the catalyst of man's evolution.

For is it not the nature of game to teach game, to evolve to its final evolution.

Until there is no need for game?

The Same

We, the same, yet different.
Flesh, blood and bones encased in colorful clay shells
of earth tones.
Positive and negative reflections that attract out of
attraction, that attract out of curiosity.
As our worlds collide, repelling or merging we
concentrate on the different, forgetting the same.
Caught up in no win sophisticated games of survival.
If continued will lead to extermination of both.
There will be no winner.
You see we do not exist we co-exist.
Difference is what makes us whole, and the same is
what allows us to survive as humanity.
Do we both not need air?
Do we both not defecate?
Do we both not decompose?
Do we both not need the warmth of love?
Do we both not feel the need to be needed?
We are different, yet the same.
Yet in humanity resides more good than evil.
Failsafe mechanisms preventing the madness of
doomsday.
Preventing the madness of co-self annihilation.
Yet we constantly push the gauntlet.
With war being the one insanity that the power
brokers agree upon.
With all chasing the concept of peace to mankind.
Yes we are the same but different.

Waiting

That night it rained, rained, and rained.
I waited for you.
From gentle mist, slow drizzle, to a windswept raging
downpour.
I paced my window looking, waiting for you.
Waiting to see the brightness of your beautiful smile.
Waiting to wipe your rain soaked eyes.
Through the haze of watery lights, the loud silence of
splashing rain wind bent leaves.
Looking looking, looking into cars, buses taxis.
The dance of lighting, the music of thunder, watery
images of
women walking towards yet away from me.
I waited for you.
I did not see you approach.
I waited and waited, pacing and pacing.
Thinking of all humanly possible excuses.
Still I waited for you to walk through the door.
Umbrella hat, coat dripping, soaking wet.
Greeting me with that wondrous smile as I wiped the
rain off your brow.
Tasting visions of you anticipating a softer reality.
I waited for you, I waited for you.
The lighting flashed a million veins across the sky.
The thunder erupted silencing all.
And you never came.
In my mind I still see your smile.
Time has padded this wound and I have moved on, but
never away from you.
Yet each time it rains.
I think of you, with each drop still waiting on you.
Because I still love you.

Laughter

Laughter, a universal language.
The spirit of mankind.
An elixir of energy that needs no translation.
Laughter, the most laid back primitive form of love.
Sneaking inside, touching heart.
Triggering facial expressions into outburst of
momentary happiness.
Laughter, the original drug.
Releasing electrochemical stimuli dancing off the
goodness inside.
Laughter, a watery burst of sunshine.
Drenching, bridging humanity towards its final global
goal.
Peace to be shared with laughter.

Last Times

Man, these last times.
More than a bitch of a burden on my soul.
They bes like a timeless journey into limbo.
Suspending reality as time fluxes.
Sending me into gigantic spirals.
Progressing, regressing, hustling, demanding,
revolving.
Taking, giving.
And I'm always needing a different same kinda change.
Yeah Man.
These last times.
Like, sometimes times bes moving with flashes of
hope, illusions of better times.
Then getting jammed from the inconsistencies within.
Or 'cause that's just the way shit jumped off that
day.
A frightening grip on reality.
Moving me, to ask the ultimate question.
Why should I ask, why am I here anyway?
I mean.
It's like I'm always looking for a way out.
Looking for something out of nowhere.
To get me over the hump.
And the next, and the next.
Now, I know that wishing don't cost you nothing.
It comes with birth and death.
But.
It's just like my mama use to say.
JR, wish in one hand and shit in the other.
See which one gets full first.
And.

If that wish comes true.
Then you'd better squeeze the hand with the shit in it.
Make sure it's real too.
It's like sometimes, I feel I'm evaporating into nonsensical repetitions.
Going somewhere, which is nowhere.
Trapped in a prison of certain uncertainties.
Now, now don't get me wrong.
Thinking I'm just ranting, raving, complaining, and bitching.
Cause I done had some better times.
It's just these last times that's like a yo-yo.
Up, down and hesitating on that thin line.
Dancing between insanity and reality.
And I bes falling both ways.
At the same time.
Yeah man, these last times.
Crushing all sense of direction into no direction.
Always bringing new tomorrows with yesterday's sorrows.
And I'm always wishing for a better tomorrow.
Cause all I know is this.
Tomorrow gone be a bitch.

Listen to Her Scream

Earth, third planet from the sun, a utopia spinning in space.
Home of the human race.
Nature, an ancient grand lady.
But lately, we've been treating her awful shady.
We dig deep into her bowels.
Extracting diamonds, copper, iron, gold.
Who knows how many other precious organs we've stole?
As we continue to mount an unpayable toll.
We choke her lungs.
Pumping tons of deadly poison in the air.
Doing it without any reasoning or care.
With floating, deadly dark clouds of acid rain.
Will the birth of future generations be in vain?
We're depleting the ozone layer, layer for layer.
As if we were some kinda ozone slayer.
Without this filtration for radiation.
Living could become a serious situation.
We're constantly cracking, breaking her bones.
Cutting away the great rain forest as if they were our own.
The Amazon, we strip, destroy.
As if it were a privileged child's wooden toy.
We dress, undress, redress her all in the name of progress.
This bountiful virgin land we rape, pillage and devastate.
As if it were a mortal enemy we're trying to annihilate.
We drain magnificent wetlands.
We constantly destroy tons of lush greenery.
Now, this must truly be an act of insanity.

For, it's intake of carbon allows us to be.
With each disappearing acre of life giving land.
She does something beyond the understanding of man.
She screams with agony and pain.
Only to fall on the ears of the deaf and vain.
We dump sludge, garbage, damn near anything.
Into waters that were once so pure, so clean.
That one-day drinking water will only be a rich man's dream.
Her children from the unseen to the majestic whale.
May become stuff of bedtime stories and fairy tales.
You see, they flirt on the brink of extinction.
As we continue to wipe them out with unbiased distinction.
We are racing damn near to the point of no return.
Yet, how many more lessons must we learn?
Nature was created with the love of perfection.
With the ability to heal, reheal and adapt to un-natural disfiguration.
You see, we need to dwell deep into ecology.
A fact that even blind men see.
Even Mother Nature has limits she can't go past.
And if we don't listen, it will be the end of man's multi colored ass!

Merry Christmas

This most festive of seasons.
Will someone please explain its reasons?
For 11 months we go about our daily routine.
And on that twelfth month, we got the damn nerve to dream.
Of peace on earth, good will towards men.
As we hustle about committing our daily sins.
We make December a month of joyous celebration.
While we struggle with visions of human liberation.
With renewed intensity.
We give with the sincerest of sympathy.
We get involved with the hopeless, the helpless, the homeless.
Those stuck in the mire of deprivation.
Will this one day of giving change their situation?
Is this the only time we give with an abundance of charity?
When we know, these needs are not a once a year rarity.
With hyper enthusiasm we celebrate the birth of Christ.
Even those we dislike, we treat nice.
We grin; pretend with motions of gifts, hugs, and kissing.
While love for humanity, now that's what's missing.
We sing songs, shake chimes, ring bells.
Next month we will tell those we helped.
Go straight to hell.

Through years of changing truths, shifting dates.
Celebration of his birth is no longer an act of faith.
Some scholars say his birth is spring.
So where did they get this wintertime thing?
But not to get involved in religion.
Cause its beliefs simply blind faith in decisions.
Christmas is mass media marketing manipulation.
Guise for financial libations.
The crowning heights of capitalism.
The last quartile incentive of commercialism.
Whatever ideology you embrace.
This Christmas shit is a slap in the face.
I hope, I pray that this wave of humanity last for more than a day.
Like Jesus said, it is better to give than receive.
So, Merry Christmas, Happy New Year.
To us fools.

Arm to Disarm

War existed with the creator willing self out of
nothingness into spirit.
War existed before the birth of and with the beginning
of time.
It is catalytic essence in fire of creation, time in
motion.
And all creations its children.
War existed in the heavens, before and with the rise
of man.
War existed in the Garden, Adam, Eve and Satan.
War began on Earth with Cain killing Abel.
And we have not stopped yet.
In nature war is supreme.
Necessary clashes of evolution that are death and
procreation.
In man, war is a baffling, bubbling confusion of self-
destructive nonsensical preservation.
Ignited by demons with meaningless definitions,
justifying, explaining hate for his fellow man.
In man war is flamed with the absence of humility.
Smoldering flashpoints of becoming selfish, acquiring
power, greed and opulence.
A dark side that resides in all of us.
Subjected to subliminal motivating thoughts of man's
ideologies.
Motivated to committing the ultimate
transgression.
The needless slaughter of man for man's ideologies.
A quest, a goal no matter how glorified, no matter
how pristine its ideals are still fueled by man's
selfishness.
Is this the true nature of man waging war?
Or is war man's plea, as he cries out for love?
Seeking prenatal warm engulfing love.

Is it his screams, his bellows of a need to be needed.
The affirmation of I am that I am.
The affirmation that I exist off the existence of
others.
Is war his reaching out to the oppressed, to abolish
tyranny, to dispose of the ruthless rule of man?
To bring social reform, democracy, and establish
freedom, all in the name of peace by going to war.
We arm to disarm for peace.
Then as now each war was to be the end of wars.
Then as now countless wars and conflicts rage over
the globe like thirsty bush fires.
With raging fever, we search for new ways of
destruction, inventing devices beyond description of
devastation.
With one device, being able to wipe out the planet 10
times over.
Yet we stockpile them as if they were becoming an
extinct species, telling others that they can't have
any toys of destruction.
And if you have any destroy them.
As if this contradiction were the answer to peace.
With arrogance we continue threatening to wipe out
the new wipe out with more power.
Is this the logic that will prevent Doomsday?
Is progress man's true insanity?
So with great certainty.
We arm to disarm, to do no harm.
We all agree to the great lie.
Doomsday devastation is the answer for peace.
Look at how far we have not come.
As for arming to disarm in the name of peace, there is
some sanity in this confusing contradiction.
However we are not hopeless.
Just desperately in need of love.
The real arm to disarm.

Works on Women

Loneliness

I sit isolated in a small room.
Staring expressionless into four bleak walls of
timeless silence.
Painfully thoughts of you flow from within.
Remembering, wishing, trying to forget.
All the emotions you had touched so deeply in my
world.
For girl, I had loved you with intensity beyond myself.
Possibly more than life itself.
Now in the darkness, loneliness, anger, rage,
bitterness.
Swells fills the depths of my very being.
Hating myself the world.
Capturing today's freshness with yesterday's
bitterness.
In solitude, chest heaving up, down.
Tears trickling into rolling down my face.
Slowly, I wipe them away.
Putting face, into hands into, oblivion.

Narcotics

Gratification the essence of pursuing existence.
It craves the feeling of good.
Pleasurable stimuli's gratifying needs of euphoria.
A survival mode, innate in all creation.
The need to feel good ensuring survival of the species.
In liquid warmth evolving without thoughts of
selfishness.
Every need attended to.
The purest of gratification.
Floating in a warm beautiful dark, bright light before
the bright dark light of birth.
Bright, brighter, brightest lights cold, wet, dry bright
darkness taking away comforts of dark brightness of
warm watery serenity.
Senses amplified bombarded assaulted, with sounds
and sights of entry into life.
The need for stimuli to gratify, to feel good, to taste
familiarity is at its greatest, as confusion reigns
supreme in an alien environment.
We panic, seeking the comfort of mother.
Remembering the smells, the sounds, and the
vibrations of her warmth.
Her flesh to your flesh, skin-to-skin, positive to
negative.
The external juice to euphoria, the link has been
established.
She is the stimulus that gratifies the continuum.
She is your first narcotic.

To Touch You

I have watched and I have waited.
Mind burning with desires of touching you.
Touching, shifting soft shades of tantalizing
darkness.
Imbedded deep within eyes of your soul.
The darkness of sensuous Africa.
Reflecting warmth of centuries before.
I need to touch, to kiss the softness of your thick
nose.
To feel it's breath from flared nostrils.
As it takes in life, giving us life.
With lips needing to touch, to kiss your thick delicate
lips.
To feel their soft etched lines of the beginnings.
Slowly licking, gently sucking, biting them.
As you shape them to speak soft words.
I think of all the possibilities.
Cause girl, you see, you erect me like that.
Yeah girl, I have seen your walk.
With smooth shapely legs propelling the very essence
of you.
Nipples erect, breast swaying to motions of a gentle
stride.
I vision myself, face buried deep.
Tasting the sweet sweat of black honey.
Engulfed by the softness of more softness.
I have watched and I have waited.
Longing to touch the sensuous curves of your inviting
hips.
To glide fingers up and down feeling their plushness.
To feel the contours of their firmness.

As they slope into the thickness of your magnificent thighs.
I long to touch, to hold, to squeeze.
To play with that heart shaped space-separating thighs from you.
To lick the soft, succulent, moist lips of you.
To penetrate that secrete place in your space.
Cause girl, you see, you erect me like that.
I have watched and I have waited.
Looking at you walking away.
Jiggling with jelly, jam, jell-O rhythms.
With that boo te defying the immutable laws of the boo te.
And I shout great googlay mooglay.
If I could touch, wrap my hands around all that ass.
A roundness that defies the laws of physics.
Yeah woman, I long to touch you in all places and spaces.
To ride you this magnificent black mare.
Would give me the erection of perfection.
Cause it's like I said before.
Woman you see, you erect me like that.

B.B.W.

Big beautiful women, softest in nature.
A plush softness that is softer than whipped cream.
No words in any tongue can describe that sensation
of flesh touching the softest of flesh.
A softness without definition other than to sink into
them.
Big beautiful women.
Yawl know what I'm talking 'bout.
Talking bout dem women, way, way, way past thick.
As you sink into their softness there is something
special about them.
A cushion that cushions all of you; I do mean all of you.
Driving some men insane taking us to the land of
feathery flesh.
I mean it's like you got so much more to work with.
For instance, look at their big beautiful breast.
They smother you with softness.
Engulfing your head in a heavenly crown.
As you sink deep into the comfort of twin mounds.
With warm soft walls that deafens sound.
And a big, big girl with big, big breast I guess you can
figure out the rest.
Now dig, folk going round talking 'bout rock hard abs,
sculptured six- pack.
And some men ain't with all of that.
And those who love dem little skinny six packs.
Must ain't never ever danced in the land of the fat.
It squiggles, it jiggles, it moves, it groves.
It shakes, it quakes, it's like jam, it's like jelly.
You just got to lay your head on a big beautiful
woman's belly.
And what about those super sized thighs?
They seem to come at you from all sides.

Dimple, upon dimple, upon dimple.
You be's grabbing, gripping, parting, pushing.
Knowing this got to be the cushions of cushions.
As hands maneuver down towards the ground.
Feeling legs, soft, strong, and round.
And hands go back.
Saving almost the best for last.
You knows I got to be talking 'bout that big old soft ass.
It don't matter bout the shape, round, flat or in-between.
That much ass is an ass man's dream.
I mean ass everywhere for days and days.
And hitting it from the back.
You know that cushion is custom made.
And moving to that last juicy tidbit.
That sometimes requires spit.
What 'bout them big gorgeous lips.
Thick, fat, juicy, and yeah I trips.
Cause seems like them lips stretch from navel to asshole.
Pussy lips everywhere, with the smell of sweet funk in the air.
And you know what you gone do.
And when you through.
You move to go deep inside.
Knowing with this cushion, it's gone be one hell of a ride.
And when you spit, it's the ultimate hit.
Coming and falling into softness at the same time.
You know that gone blow up yo' mind.
And I'd like to say.
Big beautiful women, it's bout more than a sexual play.
Out in the world in places and spaces.
They do have the cutest of faces.

Beautiful smile and a soft warm grin.
It shows the bigness of their hearts within.
Their treatment of their man is second to none.
Big Beautiful Women.
An incredible, sensuous journey of softness of flesh.
In conclusion I'd like to say.
It's a known fact.
That once you go fat.
You never go back.
Peace out big girls.

Chocolate Lady

I saw you, a deep dark chocolate lady of
unadulterated sensuality.
An alluring vision beyond my wildest dreams.
From first glance, it was apparent evident and
understood.
I wanted you to melt in my mouth, and not in my
hands.
In my mind's eye I had already tasted
your chocolate-ness.
Strong, fiery, full of dark passion.
Yeah I wanted some of that mind and body.
So I keep peeping at you.
You possessed a close-cropped, curly nappy 'fro.
A slightly thick nose, with thick melting juicy lips.
Big light bright sand brown eyes.
Shaped like angular saucer plates of smooth
chocolate magnetism.
My imagination ran wild with devilish thoughts.
I thought odd but heavenly kinda cute.
The walk, now that's what got my attention.
Not really a walk, yet more than a soulful strut.
Strutting, on legs that were silky smooth, from ankle
to thigh, shaped to the ultimate perfection.
I mean your walk was natural alluring sensuality.
Strolling, rolling those big sleek curved hips,
complimented by a flirting, flowing, twisting glide,
that accented your 360 degrees of backfield into
innocent, fluidic motions of hypnotic enticement.
Up front your luscious breast like firm, soft, juicy
melons.
Moving swaying, up, down, like they had twin,
independent
suspension.

Your lovely nipples standing at direct attention.
I thought different and damn she's so sexy.
Chocolate lady chocolate lady please melt in my
mouth, and not in my hands please.
Then I heard your voice, your laughter, sounding
melodious.
Soothing, touching places spaces, feeling good inside.
We had a conversation; your spirit was pure elation.
It was more than justification for these warm
sensations.
And I'm a just thinking she's just waiting to melt, drip,
cover,
coat somebody's body with such sweet, sweet, wet
deep dark,
rich black chocolate.
With your center of gravity, being the door to the
mother-load of chocolates.
Eh chocolate lady, please melt in my mouth,
And not in my hands
Damn chocolate lady,
Please melt in my mouth and not in my hands please?

Works on Creativity

The Artist

Artist, we tend to be weird.
Seemingly self absorbed in our own insanity.
Here, but always somewhere else.
Sensing different dimensions hidden within the
norms.
Occupied with flights of self-indulgence, while angels'
sing to our minds, tidbits of other wordily possible
impossibilities.
Artist, we be forever caught up in the mad
chaotic-ness of molding raw fire.
Struggling to unlock doors, to re-work all the rules,
that will be broken to make the senses of the heart
feel the art.
Beating, pounding, shaping unshapable imperfections
into earthly manifestations.
As the art becomes the personalities of our life
experiences.
Taking the art, inside us, inside life.
Taking the fire of art to all that is, to all that is you.
Yeah, we do tend to be out to lunch, breakfast, and
dinner too.
At times arrogant, shy, running the gauntlet of
emotions at the speed of the future creations.
Until art becomes reasons for existence.
Taking us sometimes where we should not go.
Taking us sometimes where we need to go.
To move the art to where it is neither prostitution
nor self-absorbing.

To capture the conciseness of the mass's.
To have their senses opened to what is hidden within.
To have them no longer afraid of the unknown.
A tiring process that demands you, your soul, your spirit.
Draining all emotions as you reach for the rareness of creating from the heart.
A constant turbulence of critical acclaim, finical gain, or being considered outright insane.
A journey best taken by madmen who still marvel at the wonders of creation.
As works, are deemed, works of art, classics.
Long, long after your dust has turned to dust.
So with that said I guess we have a right to be all of the above and then some.

Music

They say it was the music that drove him to the
perfection of madness.
Wildfire that consumed the very essence of his being.
Air, water, food, these, these were not his nectar.
Music, its infinity of watery waves of sounds.
These were his calling to life.
He would bend them like beams of life shaping
heartbeats.
Producing different notes from the same note.
Producing different sounds, from the same sound.
A gathering so immense, so complex.
It occupied, preoccupied him with no time for himself.
They say it was the music.
That made him hum, sing, talk to himself.
At times screaming, shouting out loud to himself, by
himself.
Going into trances.
Hearing grasshoppers jumping, dancing off blades of
grass.
Creating beats of nature, slicing through the winds of
rhythms.
They say it was the music that made him say.
Listen, please listen.
This is creation, the whats, the hows, the whys.
The mysteries of existing.
Infinite progressions of mathematical waves.
The answer to the answers.
They say it was the music.
That made him break down, crying, sobbing like a child
reaching for the comfort of its mother.
The womb of warm creativity.
The source of natural waves of sounds.

Seeking perfection of notes, before and after notes.
A journey at times would last days, weeks, months.
Negating all.
Searching for those elusive notes of celestial
harmony.
The heartbeat itself.
They say it was the music.
That made him sit at the piano for hours into days on
end.
Chain smoking, chain drinking chain thinking.
Composing, arranging, rearranging, starting all over
again.
Manuscripts staring, talking, draining him.
Note after note, after note.
Night after night after night, taking him to an end.
That was always another beginning.
They say it was the music.
That made him lose loved ones, family and friends.
Pursuing the quest of creative rhythms and sounds.
They say it was the music.
That was a gentle wave of narcotics.
Slowly sweeping him into a wave of waves.
Warm worlds of sounds.
Soothing liquid of a mother's love.
Where all that mattered was the hit of another
addictive note.
They say it was the music.
That touched his soul ignited his spirit.
Making him dance on the surface of the sun.
Kicking rhythms of his creations of heartbeats to the
children of
man.
In the end.
They said it was the music.

That left him broke, destitute.
Dying a pauper with an unmarked grave.
They never knew of the flights of fantasy.
That music would take him.
Incredible journeys of musical imagination.
Bright as creation.
Created solely as an expression to thanking the creator.
For existing, for bestowing the gift of music in his soul.
He passed away happy.
Performing, doing what he loved.
Turning watery waves of sounds.
Into the heartbeats of mankind.

Acting

Acting.
It is the oldest profession.
A skillful art of self-manipulation.
Facial, body contortions from the norm to the abnorm.
From lying to crying to becoming whatever you need to become for whatever reasons.
Self induced realities skillfully designed to take others into your world.
The unseen, seen art of electrical imagination.
Brain and body, its basic tools.
Portraying the emotions of the human experience.
Truly a forever changing, challenging complexities of improvisations.
Speaking beyond the lines of script.
Taking the voice with its varied inflections to the play of the moment.
Going beyond the physics of physics.
Moving the body with its uncountable gestures and mannerism becoming mesmerizing.
But the best, the best, yeah they get you with the eyes.
Taking intensity to new frontiers.
Taking nothingness to new lows.
Eyes full of emotion or emotionless.
Pulling you into magnetic undercurrents, as you gladly slip into their world of ever changing images.
The eyes the seat of all that is expression.
Actors no doubt they bes good.
There are all kinds of awards for the portrayal of this art of the make believe into reel or the real into make believe.
But it is make believe.

Out here in the world of changes, out here in all this beauty, all this savageness,
In this real world the best actors are not in Hollywood, but in the hood.
Not reaping bountiful salaries.
But reaping the rewards of existing with realities of ups and downs in this thing called life.
Now dig this.
On a scale of 1 to 10.
Women are ten times better actors than men.
That's why they are called woman or wo to man.
Sisters can I get an amen.
Men, we be creatures of logic dealing with facts.
Caught up in positives and negatives.
And sometimes we just don't get it.
But women they be creatures of sensing emotions.
Living by intuition.
Dancing with the sensuality of blind faith.
Balancing on the razor edge of just knowing.
Women understand men pushing us to the greatness within,
or destroying our world.
Acting or real, she hypnotizes us.
She is the life through which life is brought forth.
She realizes has not civilization been advanced for her?
Just to please her, just to comfort her.
Just to fall into the warm wetness of her.
Of all to capture she is most desirable.
She is truly the marvel of creation.
Eyes that have nurtured the growth of man.
Eyes that can tease with passion or pain.
Her intuition allows her to more than understand man.
It allows her to be ready for the next disaster, or the next triumph.

And when it comes to sexual activity.
We men don't question if it's an act or reality.
Which sometimes is one and the same.
Cause the tender trap is just that juicy.
Just that enticing, it feels just that good.
And besides a funky pussy, I ain't never met a bad pussy in my life.
I met some so funky I couldn't juice; some so tight I couldn't get it all in and some so lose I didn't know I was in.
And whether it was tight or loose I did manage to skeet.
Cause it was hot meat.
Now here's the question.
When they scream and moan as if they enjoying the bone.
Making a brother think he really got it going on.
Standing tall, knocking fire, putting a serious hump in yo' back.
I mean they eyes be rolling to the back of they head, they bes shaking and quivering, speaking in tongue shouting your name.
My brother ever wonder is this real or is it just game?
I guess the roles can be reversed.
But I bet you that sister beat you to it first.
Life is it acting?
Or.
Is acting life?
I can only say to you my brothers ask the sisters.
Cause they know and posses the true secret's of acting.

She Dances

She dances, she dances, she dances.
Sweating, pulsating, gyrating with rawsome power.
Smooth fluid, never erratic, as if she were water.
Gracefully moving with utmost precision, wasting no energy.
She dances with the aloofness of supreme confidence.
Striding, manipulating time as if she were rhythm itself.
She dances, she pounces, prancing, springing, gliding, at times flying as if gravity did not exist.
She stalks rhythm with the powerful agility of a magnificent cat.
At times defining rhythm in space.
Plugging into the heartbeat of pulsating rhythms as they touch
her sensuality.
As they touch her sexuality touching us.
She dances, she dances, eye's rolling, moaning, groaning, dripping, sweating, breast dancing to the call of rhythms.
Nipples protruding, shaking ass, rolling hips.
Stretching, spreading arms legs.
Sweat shinning, glistening on skin like black gold.
She dances, she dances, she dances.
She dances into trances taking her into flooding orgasms of the heartfelt.
Making us feel good about the rhythm of life, feel good about ourselves.

Yes, this is her life, a manifestation of time itself.
She dances, she dances, she dances.
Realizing losing one's self is getting closer to
creation.
For, she knows we are but cosmic dust.
She dances, she dances, she dances.
Seeking that plane of creativity where creativity is no
longer needed.
Only movement of thought.
She dances, she dances, she dances.
Always dancing, in her sleep, in her daydreams, in her
nightdreams, she dances.
She dances, she dances, she dances.
Dreaming, pulsating her way to creation.
To become one with the creator, yeah she dances.

To Be the Creator

To be the creator.
A quest that would be man's crowning achievement of
fulfillment of insanity.
To be the architect of creation, forming nothing into
time, creating space to expand, creating existence,
to begin.
Creating all worlds, creating all that is.
Concepts that defy man's feeble logic, knowledge and
understanding of what is.
As he attempts to take what is, back to its
beginnings.
Man, simply a shell composed of earth, sprinkled with
essence of universe.
Contaminated with the sickness of ego vanity,
wanting to replace the creator with himself.
Stating with defiance, that in nature he alone is
supreme.
The ultimate egotist who visions the creator as his
last opponent.
He revels believing that his vast pinhead of knowledge
and intellect will unlock miracles of the universe and
explain phenomena of the unexplained.
That intellect takes him past Armageddon.
That he alone will sit upon the throne and pass
judgment upon the resurrection of man.
He pretends to struggle with the ethics of morals,
the dilemmas of compassion, equality and
humanness.
When he has nether ethics, morals nor compassion.
Where ethics, morals and compassion are tainted
with the corruptness of money and power.
Where equality is blatant or subliminal racism.

He is a madman racing to the edge of extinction.
In a desperate struggle of third world exploding procreation.
He dips into vast resources furthering the complexities of his technology to erase the creator.
From test tube masturbation to invitro fertilization, to cloning.
He moves deeper into the realm of accepting his own lie.
Blinded by unlocking genetic codes gene manipulation, introducing foreign stimulation, inducing mutating cell replication.
Technical data, infused with the laws of nature, have mislead man into believing that he can become the creator.
That he in fact can create some thing out of nothing.
That he in fact can create life.
He bombards himself with honors, accolades of his futile attempts to dethrone the creator.
He fills your head with the latest of scientific advancements.
Only to be confronted with more mysteries and more mysteries of the mystery he thought he had solved.
With breakneck speed he moves closer to a goal never to be attained.
He is truly Dr.Frankenstein reaching for the essence of existence.
He cannot create the reality of I am.
He will never admit this truth.
He will continue his quest to be the all in all.
And upon fulfillment of a goal never to be achieved, he will scream like in that old movie "It's alive it's alive, Igor.
Igor we have done it.
It's alive."

To Lovers Who Dance

Dancing mankind's gift to the creator.
Universal language of movements that vibrate
rhythms of life.
Transcending flourishing establishing a rhythmic flood
in all cultures.
It is non-discriminating permeating us with self
induced movements to begin the quest for the source
of all that is rhythm.
With rhythm into rhythms being the base of life,
it calls us with great expectations.
From the dance of birth to the dance of death.
It is something we all do.
It is the sound the movements of these rhythms
that motivate
pushing us to share these rhythms this feel good
with someone who loves to dance.
With someone who lives to dance.
And when lovers of dance become lovers who dance
the rhythms of creative movements.
It becomes much much more than dance.
A complexity that becomes simply physical
manifestations expressing movement seeking the
source of rhythm.
You see , you see lovers, they know they are simply
containers of earth and water that define the dance
by becoming fluid movements of elastic electricity as
they seek a path to the source of the prime vibe.
You see dancers who are lovers understand that
rhythm and dance much like themselves are life
mates and that neither can exist without the other.
With uninhibited freeness they move to rhythm that
is blind to all but rhythm.

Rhythm that exposes the raw nature of existing.
But to dance the dance of rhythms there must be a
rhythm if only the rhythm of the heart pushing feet
to dance the rhythm into rhythms into dance.
Becoming an infectious whirl wind that sweeps lovers
off their feet moving them trance like feeling its
hypnotic rhythms.
Dancing as if only, the quest of rhythm is all that
matters.
Bursting forth astounding cataclysmic fleet of foot
movement's dancing as if air were an ally.
Failing arms, twisting torso, expanding, pushing
twisting muscles into flights of primal explosion.
As if gravity tells them do it, cause baby I got your
back.
With daring boldness they move they strut until they
start to become the dance.
Until independence of movements fuse evolving into
unison of movement.
In which they become each other, becoming one.
And when lover's become one with each they move to
bond to become one with the prime rhythm that was
induced into rhythms that became creation.
This is their life's quest becoming one with rhythms of
creation.
To become orgasmic celebrating the spurting
rhythms of the heartbeat of creation.
So they dance and they dance and they dance as
they strive to become movement that is one with
creation.

Stardust Dance

Spirit creator of all.
Beginning with no beginning, ending without an end.
No concept of matter yet matter, no concept of
time, yet linear, no concept of space yet space was, is
and still expanding. Existing yet not existed.
Spirit was and was not.
A more than perplexing contradicting unexplainable
thought.
Beyond comprehension baffling us even in death.
As we seek to return to Spirit that exhaled us into
the essence of Stardust that danced into all that is.
From within the breath of Spirit with purpose of
creation.
Exhaling energy sending blinding light of spirit filled
stardust that danced dividing the darkness into
twofold.
The dark and the light dark.
Thus for all that is, the birth of Stardust Dance.
From within the breath of Spirit with purpose of
creation. Exhaling, exhaling exhaling orchestrating
seemingly random, tumultuous chaotic exploding
colors of stardust dancing into multidimensional
existence.
This magnificent erupting birth of stardust danced in
space, becoming planets, stars, moons in emptiness.
Anchoring themselves with the infinite order of spirit.
Hosting all worlds hosting all life.
Stardust Dance the dance of life.
Sparkling bits of Spirit filled cosmic dust forever
touching us forever influencing us.
We are dust of Stars, Spiritual souls dancing
journeying back the essence of essences.

Journeying back to a dance that began with Spirit timeless years in the making.
Becoming us bestowed with free will linking us with the commonality that we are products of the dust of stars.
And life the end results of a beautiful dance.
The dance is life.
Moving strutting, undaunted exhibiting all the good, the bad and the dust in between.
Personifying profoundly stating that this dance of life is forever flashing, exploding in the doorways of time.
And that through all the good the bad and sometimes the sho'nuff ugly that life is good.
This dance with life is absolute.
Like time it moves straight ahead no chaser.
Making decisions on the now.
Reaching into generation yet unborn becoming an ever evolving Stardust dance with life.
The dance like life with true flexibility is foundation from day one.
It is solid dust dancing with life and it is good.
The Stardust Dance forever changing is nothing new.
It is the sum total of all that is.
The aroma of a flower.
The sensation of a lovers touch.
In themselves are meaningless.
Nothing without the essence of the dust dance.
Yes this dust dance with life is good.
Forever expanding, yielding only to death, to become dust becoming life again.
This is the ultimate gift of the dance, life and it's variety of infinite variety.

Works on Addiction

Addiction   (The Comfort Zone)

The comfort zone.
A place offering a sanctuary of emotional support.
A friend of silent silky smooth deception.
Gliding, sliding, existing within frameworks of
selfish, arrogant, demanding, dictating, on the
moment of now desires.
The comfort zone.
It's appeasing to, the most gratifying of sensations.
The ultimate Jekell and Hyde transformation.
Stripping away reality's cohesiveness.
Enhancing the whirlwind energy of negative
stagnation.
A prerequisite, for the survival of addiction.
Self parasitic death who revels in the destruction of
self.
Destroying logic, turning self-love into self loathing.
Becoming the you that you never were, just for the
moments of pleasure for pleasure.
Cause damn, damn this shit is good, this shit is the
bomb.
Can I have another hit to hit my comfort zone?
The comfort zone.
Addiction, be it drugs or picking up bird shit with
boxing gloves.
It is isolated with insanity producing jagged edges.
Erratically cutting the fabric of time and space.
Floating becoming blind to all.
With high being purpose of life.
A high disrupting, taking control.
Prompting frantic intensive synch less search's, for
the mystical elusiveness of complete euphoria.

You know that hit that makes your brain bust a nut as you come all inside self.
As that shit takes u to a place where nothing matters but another hit.
Can I feel that good again?
Goddamnit can I feel that good forever?
Can I have another hit please?
Man all I want is a godfather.
The comfort zone.
Hey man check out this watch, gold necklace, and gold ring.
Check out these gators and I got some lizards in the trunk of my Benz.
The comfort zone.
Damn it can I have another hit please.
I just wanna get with this freak you know and freak off.
I even got the title to the Benz.
Come on man you know I'm good and look at how much money I done spent.
The comfort zone.
Intoxicants addicting shooting past speed of light to the center of the pleasure center.
Endorphins spiraling, spinning, flipping out of control.
Brain feeling body saying, what the fuck is this?
Like some shit you never had before.
But after that first trip in space.
That intensity of that sensation you ain't gone never feels no mo.
But fuck it close enough is close enough.
While it slowley dulls, numbs, and induces the illusion of the illusions of utopia.
Goddamn it can I have another hit please please?
Don't you wanna take a look at this shit I got?
The comfort zone.
Puff, shoot, snort, drink relax.

A realm of thoughts of nothing but high.
We, you and I, will satisfy ourselves until there is
nothing left.
Addicting you into nothingness.
To the comfort zone.
And when I'm through I'll move on.
Yelling to Scottie, beam me up another
motherfucking addict.
Cause like you said my man Goddamnit, Jesus fucking
Christ,
This shit is the bomb; this shit is a whip.
Scotty hurry up with that host please.

Lady of the Night

The strain of years, of consuming intoxicants etched
themselves deeply upon her face.
They had taken their toll.
Eyes, no longer crystal clear full of life, no longer
bright, or shinning.
Now lifeless, cloudy, dull, reddish yellow.
Desperately searching for real love of understanding.
Her teeth, no longer perfect or white.
Stained, yellow to brown, decayed, worn away.
Broken, like the dreams she might have once had.
Lips painted thick fire red.
Attempting to hide cracking, splitting skin of lips
that no longer held any sensuality.
Her face, no longer glowing, supple, smooth or sleek.
Its skin dotted potholes discoloration and bold deep
wrinkles that arrived twenty years too early.
Hands, arms, ankles showing the abuse of the years.
Swollen, littered with tracks and abscesses.
Leading to other tracks and new abscesses.
Her once fine frame ravaged by her search for
Shangri-La.
The blows, rocks and alcohol eagerly feeding itself on
her.
Eating legs, hips, ass, breast.
Into a frame of sagging, wrinkled flesh.
Still she parades herself.
Offering a dilapidated tender trap that has become
desensitized.

Through the misuse of overuse, of constant abuse.
Her lips, tongue, mouth, jaws, tired of sucking,
tasting, smelling
odors that reek with damn, I've become numb to this.
Yet, she goes on surviving, she moves, she grooves.
Seeking love in all the wrong places.
Submerging the logic of truth.
Silently in the stillness of night space she screams.
Another rock, another drink.
You think?
Another blow, another john to go!

Chronical

James diverted our attention to the flat surface of the
sink.
On it a shot glass, a butter knife, and a bottle of Bo Peep
ammonia. He went into his pocket, came out with a bag of
flake shell soft rock, tore a chunk off, put it in a shot glass.
He put a teaspoon of water a little ammonia. He began to
work the butter knife back and forth in the bottom of the
glass.
The cocaine went from slimy oil,
to snot into white rocks sticking to the knife.
He crushed the rocks, reached in the cabinet above,
got a glass with a nylon stocking on it.
Put the powder on top, got a glass of water,
poured it over the stocking.
Laughing, he said gotta rinse the ammonia off or that shit
or it will slowly kill you.
He handed me a pipe, a torch,
which consisted of a broken hanger with a ball of cotton
wrapped tightly around it.
He then gave me a large amount of cocaine,
later to be called a godfather.
He explained how I should hit it, don't swallow it,
hold it in your lungs,
push it up to your brains.
He then dipped the torch into some grain alcohol,
handed me the torch and lit it.
I was to learn later that the grain burned clean
and didn't affect the taste of the cain.
I said ok, and hit that shit just like I smoked herb.
I hit that pipe, shocking those around
'cause I made a pretty thick white cloud in the bowl
and then sucked it all in.
The pipe was crystal clear. Empty.
They thought I was going to choke and spit my guts
up.

I held it down just like it was herb, and when I could no longer hold I exhaled.
Man goddamn, what the fuck is this?
There are no words to describe this sensation.
All I knew was that I wanted me another hit.
Dick got harder than a motherfucker.
I shoulda gotten the first indication that this shit wasn't right when I went to piss.
After smoking hit after hit, after hit
and drinking beer I had to take a leak.
I went into the washroom, unzipped and went to grab myself
and missed,
I grabbed again and nothing,
I panicked, grabbed again and found a nub,
this shit has taken my dick back into my navel tap dancing on my spine.
As I damn near pissed down my pant leg.
But fuck that, 'cause I still wanted me some mo.
So we smoked some mo. Don and I left.
I got the second indication when I got home.
I had smoked to the point of no hard on.
I wanted to jam my old lady but I couldn't.
Not only had my dick shrunk, I couldn't even get a hard on.
I could not sleep that night,
was deep tripping into the world of the why's and what ifs,
zoning into the no answers of death,
I was terrified.
Questioning why was I born to die,
the kind of shit that drives people crazy.
I said ain't nothing supposed to make a man act and feel like that.

Think these spaced out thoughts.
I ain't never gone smoke that shit again.
The next night i was there, mesmerized,
watching, puffing, sweating,
a madman looking for a freak 'fo i lose the stiffness,
looking for a freak to bow to the godhead
if i hadn't smoked too much of that shit.
Thus began a journey of 20 plus years of waste.

Works on the Struggle

Invisible Man

I am the invisible man.
Not science fiction, nor of H. G. Wells imagination, but
fact.
Transparent blacknuss in white abstractions of
reality.
A vibrant live meaningful energy, with hopeless
aspirations.
I am the invisible man.
Surviving centuries of indifference and human denial.
Stairways into live exploding nightmares.
Visible repercussions of white kind's scheme dream,
for supremacy.
As I attack, attempting to rearrange a deranged
mentality.
I am the invisible man.
Trapped in a deadly drain game of mental gymnastics.
An expendable, usable, reusable, statistical test tube
soul of the 20th century search to attain godliness.
And all for the visible benefit, improvement and
propagation of white kind.
I am the invisible man.
Scholar, athlete supreme, with visible expectations
of reaching for more than invisible dreams.
For whatever towering heights I soar to attain.
To white kind, they are simply invisible gains of my
visible pain.
Yes, I am the invisible man.
From the womb to the tomb, saturated with doom
and gloom.
Clever ideologies for the destruction of this black
invisibility.

Designed for the destruction of black self-esteem.
To keep us out of the visible scheme of things.
To take us to annihilation or assimilation.
Siphoning this invisible power to the white nation.
I am, I am the invisible man.
This jet-black, blue-black invisibility that now
threatens white folk visible reality.
I am the invisible man.
And I am mad as hell, 'cause you see, I am the root; I
am the root from which human life has sprung.
Yet, I remain firmly entrenched on the bottom rung.
My invisibility confirms my right to be.
You see, even his history hails, proclaims.
This black shinned, nappy headed, big nose, big-lipped
man.
From the womb of Mother Africa, as the father,
The father of mankind.

European American Blacknuss

We cannot deny what we have become.
Reflections of free insanity that is a world power.
No longer Africans.
Roots are linkages to a distant past of greatness,
never to be ignored or denied.
All that is now came out of darkness.
Leaving us legacies of roots of beginnings whose
foundations are entrenched in Earth.
We are a unique.
We have never been Europeans.
Who emptied her jails into the New World becoming
America.
Europeans who showed their feelings of freedom, by
enslaving us into circles of slavery.
Euro America moved into greatness without remorse,
insensitive to our screams for the right to be human.
Even after the great Emancipation we were never
accepted as immigrants, who became Americans as
they melted in the melting pot.
In that melting pot we were boiled.
Sinking to the bottom as others tread upon our
foundations.
History speaks only too well of this fact.
We are a unique.
Surviving four centuries of non-ending bombardments
of genocide, genocidal assimilation, forever fighting
this constant pressure of unyielding oppression.
Yielding four centuries of innovative, cross-cultural
adaptations, while maintaining the fact that us
simply being us, we are forever black.
No longer African, never European, never American.
Mutating into uniqueness.

So what do I put on the application.
Other, now what is other suppose to be or mean?
We have run the gamete of the name game in terms
of defining who we are.
We have called ourselves all shades of darkness.
Yet we run past ourselves, ignoring the truth of who
we are.
Like diamonds mutating into this uniqueness under
constant pressure of unrelenting oppression.
We are Black by design, European by unyielding forces,
and Americans by birthright.
So what do I put on the application, Black
Euroamerician?
They say fit in where you can get in; get in where you
can fit in.
God knows we try.
We are caught up in balls of contradictions.
No matter how much knowledge we have of Africa,
how African we dress, walk, talk, eat, and sleep.
Even our thoughts no matter how close to home.
We are contaminated with the american way of life.
We cannot get away from the fact that we are a
product of this insanity.
Our lifestyle no matter how innovative they still
reflect,
Blacknuss of Africa, reflecting into Europe, into
America.
It's like skin no matter how hard some folk try; they
just can't get away from it.
We as black folk live in a multitude of adaptations.
Confronted with the constant stigma of defining who
we are.

The list of slings and arrows we sling at each other is endless.
Curare tips of slow polarization, polarizing, lulling us away from the truth.
We truly are a product of this insanity.
We are what we are.
A clashing merging of cultures.
And if we continue to pit ego of stupidity with ignorance, against ego of stupidity with more ignorance.
If we continue to look at the difference's without understanding there's no difference.
Which is the ultimate divide and conquer.
We shall be like the myth of the lemmings rushing over the cliffs to destroy themselves.

House Niggers-N-Field Niggers

House niggers-n-field niggers and yes Uncle Toms.
Black men and women the foundations of bridges
between slavery and survival.
Remaining unheralded in any written history.
Hell who's ever done a term paper a thesis a Doctoral
or any kind of paper on them as whole in terms of
their magnificent contributions to the survival of
black people?
House niggers-n field niggers and yes even Uncle
Toms.
Some were mesmerized by the manipulation of
Christianity.
Some possessed by a serious fear of death but
couldn't wait to die to go to a white heaven.
Some just loved white folk dirty draws becoming
straight up Uncle Toms.
U know massa sick, we sick too.
They became believers of their own lies.
Forgetting Africa latching on to what is the now.
To be captive and living dead is better than free and
dead.
And Uncle Tom a known ass kisser assured his
progeny would survive and that's why his breath
always smelled like shit.
Cause of them house niggers-n field niggers and yes
even Uncle Toms we still here.
You see u were either with us or against us depending
on the role u played
Some house niggers, some field niggers and yes even
some Uncle Toms were straight up real niggers in the
woodpile.
You know, hiding in the woodpile waiting to bust
massa head.

They detested slavery, plotted for freedom.
They didn't give a fuck 'bout whiteness 'bout the massas white god.
Or any of that shit that alienated him from Africa.
They held on to the blacknuss of Africa.
To be dead and free is better than being captive and a slave.
Cause of them brothers-n-sisters we still here.
House niggers'-n field niggers and yes Uncle Toms.
Never knowing which is which.
They played the ultimate game of cat and mouse.
From, ye'sah massa, to smiling white teeth, to bowing down.
To ground glass, stolen books, implanting seeds of revolution.
These black people plotted, mapping ideas changing the course of black-kind.
They were the sparks of light birthing freedom's revolution.
Yet, no one speaks of them.
So to dem house niggers-n field niggers and to my uncle tom.
Who still exist, us never knowing which is which?
I recognize the importance of your lives.
You are reasons why we continue to survive.
To you my brothers and sisters.
My hat comes off, my heart goes out.
Cause no doubt, cause of you.
We still here.

The Ship's Gut

Genocidal assimilation was with us in the ships gut.
Tap dancing with razor heels on inhumane conditions.
Laying down rhythms that cut tongues of defiance.
Stabbing the heart in its struggle for freedom to be
human.
A demon planting seeds of lies twisting the history of
us omitting the greatness of us.
With surgical precision radically cutting changing
leaving a permanent scar of distain of hatred for us in
the New World.
Genocidal assimilation was with us in the ships gut.
A slow deathful journey with survivors being oblivious
to the pains of terrors that waited in the New World.
A World spewing hate for us.
As strong as time progressing, as consistent as
space expanding.
A World of stiff cold nonflexible rhythms that
established rules for our existence in your reality.
Simply put they were to worship you as superman, to
worship a white god who was most forgiving and
would reward you only if you died and went to a white
heaven.
But most important to believe that we are much
much less than you.
Genocidal assimilation was with us in the ships gut.
Floating to this New World with us becoming
backbones that were trodden upon as others chased
and built the American schemes of their dreams.
With us being one of the major catalysts that helped
catapult America into her greatness.
Catapulted her into becoming the great capitalist
and entrepreneurs whose fortunes are rooted in our
blood of generations long ago.

Generations whose legacies are dust of bones forgotten, hidden or simply blown away with the passage of time.
Genocidal assimilation was with us in the ships gut.
Docking, dumping us into a vile world that still denies us the rights of human existence.
Docking, dumping us into a world that still attempts to take our breaths away in the womb.
And still we seek the equality, respect and humanness in a world where we are hated for simply being as all mankind are, Gods most stunning creations.
Hated by those who say they believe in the reality of the creator. Those who preach the gospel of humanity and who with great zeal profess to spread the brotherhood of love.
Those who scream with great embellishments that all men are created equal.
Genocidal assimilation was with us in the ships gut.
Constantly evolving deluging us with the most adaptive, innovated, improvisational genocidal techniques thought of.
Birthing forth sophisticated schemes of social cultural, and economic deprivation fasting themselves upon us.
Attacking embryos to the elderly sparing no one in its implementation of this massive genocidal scheme of assimilation.
Yet we defy exponential odds.
Refusing to become a footnote on a footnote.
Refusing to become extinct.
And still do you not understand black is truly beautiful.
It is this beauty that has allowed us to survive.

Does this beauty in us frighten you?
Does this beauty in us confuse you?
Genocidal assimilation was with us in the ships gut.
Our voices were not heard as we screamed for human rights.
Four centuries later still we are not respected as human beings.
We are still lynched, still treated less than human.
We are like an itch you that you scratch, scratch and scratch that keeps on itching and itching and itching.
The harder you scratch the more you hurt yourself as well as me.
And as we as a mass of people move from imitation of whiteness.
Becoming knowledgeable of the greatness of us.
Never realizing, understanding that we are the heartbeat of creation.
The rippling effect of the ships gut shall always haunt us, never hurting us.
But, to constantly remind us, of the greatness of us.

U-Lie the 4th   (Independence Day)

Days before U-Lie the 4th.
We break to the store.
Buying food, spirits, drugs by the ton.
Getting ready for this party to come
We buy something new to wear.
Fix our face, our hair, as we prepare.
To celebrate independence.
Now for black folk does this make any sense?
We sit waiting for smoky illusions.
Of freedoms cloudy confusion.
We party harder than those who enjoy fruits of this freedom.
Celebrating what white folk think they alone have won.
As we speculate, debate, wait for equality to come.
We bath in glory of living beyond shackles and chains.
To reap the glory of our father's forgotten gains.
To frolic in the land of free, home of the brave.
As white folk laugh, saying this is the way it's gone be played
Cause don't dem niggers know they still slaves.
We induce their minds with sparks of harmonious racism.
As we keep their minds in bar-less prisons.
We'll even join them for that u-lie 4th celebration.
This freedom thing gots to have black and white participation.
We'll even elect them to public office with imaginary ascension.
Never to mention the ass they gone be kissing.

On U-LIE THE 4th politicians spit speeches of fire and brimstone.
As they attempt to cover up their wrongs of doing wrong.
Preaching, expounding.
The virtues of voting, democracy, capitalism.
Never explaining, these are the building blocks of racism.
With ever expanding bases of economic prisons.
Producing waves of powerless decisions.
Six walls closing from all directions.
As politicians make beds of lies for the next election.
On U-Lie the 4$^{th.}$
White folk shore up the lies and schemes.
As they scream.
Black folk reach for the American Dream.
Be all you can be.
But you niggers ain't never gone be free.
On U-Lie the 4th we forget the misery of a painful history.
The carnage, dehumanization and raping of the black nation.
We tend to forget, on that u lie 4th celebration.
Pretending we've made it in that circle of independence.
While in reality we still peeping.
Attempting to straddle, to cross the fence.
On U-Lie the 4th the air is thick with the smell of bar-b-que.
Fireworks exploding into a gala of brilliant lights.
As we celebrate this nations primal freedom fight.
The over indulgence of food, drink, and drugs.
All in the name of a declaration.

That spit forth the birth of the idea of a free nation.
That puts black folk in precarious situations.
It states that all men should be treated with
equality.
To enjoy the freedom of humanity.
That we all are the same.
But that's some mo of that U-Lie the 4th game.
So, again i ask you freedom,
For black folk, when will it come?
Hey man.
Could I have a piece of that bar-b-que?

Grabbing Myself

White folk always wonder.
Why black men be grabbing, holding on to themselves.
And I bet to this day they aren't got a fucking clue.
You see you, got to go back to the beginning to
understand this.
In the beginning you forced yourself upon my woman.
Abusing her in the name of God and Christianity.
Delegating her to become the recipient of your rapes,
your sodomy your sick ass perversion.
Taking with ferocity that which should be given freely.
You had become God and Satan almighty.
Ha-ha yes but your woman she waited with the
curiosity of lust.
She waited lurking in darkness to give herself to
darkness.
For just as her man she was fascinated by the beauty
of this new raw black sexuality.
She waited to see if the rumors of myth were true.
Waiting anticipating salivating for its thickness to
invade her.
To make her scream with passions of lust.
Just as her husband had screamed as he poured
himself into the chattel he held captive.
She waited to become orgasmic as never before.
Waiting risking death for a taste of blackness.
To get the white cream that comes from blackness
to taste to suck this forbidden fruit.
For black men it was truly power, the power of black
sexuality.

This grabbing, this holding on to simply a declaration
of the power of black sexual manhood.
Any other grasping for power were simply
transparent illusions.
Before we left the Motherland you started killing me to
steal from me.
Birthrights, legacies, culture, religion, my woman,
my children, anything that personified my greatness.
Over the centuries you have stolen everything.
An obsession at which you have became quite
proficient.
You have stolen all but the soul of my improvisations of
existing in a space of contradicting contradictions.
Your conscious is oblivious to destruction of others, to
establish the fact that you are the shit.
Remembering the fact that you are a thief I thought
about myth you white folk had established,
You know the one once you go black you never go back.
But I figured old boy hanging low was pretty safe.
I then thought about the decadent and perverted
society in which we live.
In terms of achieving sexual pleasure we are at an all
time high.
And with the constant onslaught of the ever
expanding technology of organ transplantation.
This could become a freighting situation.
Hearts, livers, lungs, kidneys, intestines, pancreas,
eyeballs.
Shit who knows what organ is next my dick and balls?
Besides the brain we know what the next biggest sex
organ is.

So armed with that point of view I figured to your killing, stealing, taking self you would be true,
It would be just a matter of time before transplant technology would shine, chop off yours and give you mine.
And once again remembering the fact that you are a thief so slick with the art of stealth stealing.
Every now and then I just gotta grab myself.
Just a grabbing and a holding and a squeezing just jacking myself up.
Just checking making sure nuts and dick are still there.
Or as white people say:"My penis and testicles".
You know still in one piece.
Now white folk that's why I be's grabbing myself.

The Rainbow Coalition

Black Women, fibers of light.
Brilliant, blinding at times subduing.
A rainbow of hues from high yellow.
To ultra high yellow, to damn near white.
Dipping into the multi shades of blacknuss.
Chocolate, caramel, tan, paper bag brown, chestnut
brown.
Dodo brown, redbone brown, cocoa brown and all its
variables.
Finally, embracing the ultimate.
That shinning, shimmering, jet black, beyond blue black.
Black women.
These are true flowers of the earth.
Rich, black, sweet, juicy, fragrant, petals of aroma.
Instilling the raw essence of inborn resistance.
A natural repellent offsetting this onslaught of
genocide.
This slight of hands assimilation.
And.
The greatest of European genocidal thinkers wonder.
How do they survive?
The coalition baby. The Rainbow Coalition.
Black women. My beautiful black queens.
Whose hearts encompasses the very definition of
space itself.
Your warm embrace radiates more sustenance than a
billion suns.
Black women.
Between your magnificent thighs of darkness.
Sprouted forth seeds destined for more than
greatness.
More than hope against these atrocities of injustice.

Key elements in the dynamic flow of your will, to
survive.
A statement.
I am all that I am and much, much, much more.
And the greatest of European genocidal thinkers.
Ponder in complete bewilderment.
How do they survive?
The Coalition Baby.
The Rainbow Coalition.
Black Women,
My beautiful black women.
Possessing an inbreed tenacity for propagation of
selfkind.
A ferocity so intense.
It motivates a unique understanding of this whole
scheme of things.
Its variables and all the hypothetical situations.
Formulated for the whole destruction of black kind.
Due to you, my black queens.
Not only do we survive, we thrive, we multiply.
'Cause you ain't gone let us die.
Yes, my black queens.
You are deeper than deep.
A stunning intricate work of reality.
A jewel, so highly polished its sole purpose of
reflection.
To mirror herself into a continuum.
Prophecy, you deemed to be fulfilled, not denied.
So let those thinkers ,think, shout, scream, foam at
the mouth.
Grind their brains until they become insane.
Cause they ain't gone never understand the
mysteries of the
Coalition.
Mysteries as deep as the mystery of life itself.
Cause it's the coalition baby.
The rainbow coalition.

Martin the King

Dreams, smoky Illusions of reality.
To be chased by those who only dream.
Martin the King did more than dream.
A giant intellect among men.
Brilliant, black cool fire in the eye of the storms.
Martin the King did more than dream.
His voice spiritual, emotional trembling thunder from
heaven.
Touching our hearts with his awareness.
Pushing us strive for perfection of humility.
While we strive towards the perfection of mankind.
From the racial insanity of separate but equal into
desegregation, into integration, into a harmonious
nation.
Dreams smoky Illusions of reality.
Martin the King did more than dream.
As all great men he grew.
Evolving and taking us to higher planes of spirituality
morality and humility.
Explaining to the world that the truths of truths are
not to be denied.
That all men are truly created equal.
Martin the King did more than dream.
No longer blinded by the tunnel vision of black and
white.
He broadened his scope of social responsibility.
He preached blistering foreign and domestic policies.
He spoke against the inhumanness of Vietnam
Fusing the rich, the middle, the poor, the
disenfranchised base of Americana into the stream
of the governmental American conciseness
Feeling the pulse touching the hearts of us all.
Martin the King did more than dream.

Gathering uniting the mass's acquiring power.
Establishing a serious base of power.
To the powers that be whoever they be this was unacceptable.
A balcony several necks covered no mistake steps back.
Hot lead sliced through the air.
Shattering dreams that were piercing smoky illusions becoming more than dreams, touching reality.
Once again the powers that be silenced the truth.
They knew that Martin the King dreams were the basis of reality of social reform a new awakening.
But we shall always remember.
I have a dream.

U Done Come A Long Way Baby

To all the Massa's, overseers, Uncle Tom's, field
niggers, house nigger's, niggers in the woodpile, nigger
lovers, nigger haters, or any other kind of nigger that
contributed to the continuum.
To all the black folk who decided to stay fight and not
run. Without u this historical era could have never
begun.
U done come a long way baby?
From the beginning of free labor to a thankless nation.
To the lies of the Great Emancipation Proclamation.
To the fears of death that evaporated.
In the fight for integration.
That led to another kind of separation.
U done come a long way baby?
To the death defying struggles of attaining manhood.
That induced a psyche that stays in an
improvisational mood.
U done come a long way baby?
To all the lye lard grease and potatoes that made
nappy hair become so called pretty and straight.
Patent leather looking hair that was escape.
To Madame Walker who got rich off the hot comb.
Right or wrong Sister Girl clocked dem dollars over a
million strong.
With grease and hot comb.
The shames of naps were gone.
U done come a long way baby?
To all the wigs weaves, extension lifts, and falls that
had sisters thinking that hair was the all in all.
To all the bushes, collagists fades, corn rows, plats
braids, afros, a cold comb, and almighty dreads.
Stating emphatically I ain't ashamed of my nappy ass
head.

U done come a long way baby.
To all the bleaching crèmes lotions and potions
designed to hide or take away our beautiful black
identity.
U done come a long way baby?
To all the folk who denounced ignorant insanity of
racial superiority?
To all the parents who showed their kids their racial
stupidity.
Showing them how not to be
U done come a long way baby?
To all the folk who taught their children that we are all
children of the creator.
With none being greater.
U done come a long way baby?
To the music to the music that soothed the pains of
this savage insanity.
Allowing us to move and groove and constantly
improve in these turbulent seas of contradicting
misery.
Allowing us to be more than they will ever see.
U done come a long way baby?
To all the dreams of that have allowed us to forget
who we are.
To all the images that have allowed us to rise above
the bar.
U done come a long way baby?
To all above I say thank you.
And with great sincerity.
For without u this historical election could never be.
For these are the times of the truths of realty.
Now as we forge ahead with great anticipation of a
history making election.
Politically we strive to move towards improving some
of humanity's imperfections.

Obama defines the crowing heights of the American political arena.
A man with an infectious charismatic demeanor.
He is the evolution of a hopeful resolution.
Knowing he is not the entire solution.
U done come a long way baby.
I mean Bush McCain both richly insane with the same game.
Obama thrives off the drama.
A genius in the legalities of law.
Maybe a flaw.
The law more revered than the bible now becomes libel.
This genius will take it to never expected expectations.
Hopefully the road to human salvation.
So as we move from one era to another.
Who would have thought that a brother would lead the charge in the chaos of America's push for a better world?
Where hopefully he will go where no Pres has dread to tread.
Allowing us to scream screams of creative phrases of jubilation laced with shouts of ecstatic elation.
Shouting to the top of the world.
Shouting to the top of the world.
U done come a long way baby.
Yeah baby u know u done come a long way baby.

One Saturday Morning

He had attended the most prestigious schools.
A Rhodes Scholar.
Reared in the lap of sheltered luxury.
Often wore blue contact lenses.
Spoke the Queens English with perfection of
whiteness.
He was the pinnacle of black success.
Because he had achieved white success.
He was impervious to the plight of blackness.
One Saturday morning, he ran out his multi-million
split-level, two-car garage, swimming pool, tennis
court, basketball court crib.
He broke out without his driver's license and no state
I.D.
That suburban cop's wore his ass out.
He screamed, he shouted, I can buy you white
motherfuckers.
They laughed and whupped his ass harder.
And when the smoke cleared.
Brother man had one hell of a lawsuit.
But, it took him until one Saturday morning.
To realize that he was still
Black.

www.ingramcontent.com/pod-product-compliance
Lightning Source LLC
LaVergne TN
LVHW011407080426
835511LV00005B/427